Jim Ratcliffe

JIM RATCLIFFE

The Industrialist Behind INEOS

Grant G. Greech

Jim Ratcliffe

All rights reserved. No part of this publication may be reproduced, distributed, or transmitted in any form or by any means, including photocopying, recording, or other electronic or mechanical method, without the prior written permission of the publisher, except in the case of brief quotations embodied in critical reviews and certain other noncommercial uses permitted by the copyright law.
Copyright © Grant G. Greech, 2024.

Jim Ratcliffe

TABLE OF CONTENTS

INTRODUCTION

CHAPTER 1: WHO IS JIM RATCLIFFE

Early life and upbringing

Early Influences: Shaping the Industrialist Mindset

CHAPTER 2: THE PATH TO INDUSTRIAL SUCCESS

The Management Consultant Years at Esso and Courtaulds

MBA at London Business School: Building Strategic Acumen

Transition into Private Equity: A New Direction

CHAPTER 3: FOUNDING INEOS

Acquiring the BP Chemicals Division: A Game-Changer

INEOS' Growth Strategy: A Focus on Cost Efficiency and M&A

The INEOS Business Model: Lean Operations, Bold Acquisitions

CHAPTER 4: EXPANDING THE EMPIRE

Global Expansion: INEOS' Operations in Europe, Asia, and America

The Ongoing Push for Growth: Major Projects and Ventures

Jim Ratcliffe

Strategic Partnerships and Joint Ventures in the Chemical Industry
CHAPTER 5: INNOVATING IN ENERGY AND BEYOND
Leadership Philosophy and Management Style
CONCLUSION

Jim Ratcliffe

INTRODUCTION

This book explores Ratcliffe's early life, from his humble upbringing in Failsworth to his education and the pivotal moments that set him on the path to success. It examines his visionary leadership, his unorthodox approach to business, and his ability to adapt to rapidly changing markets. Ratcliffe's career spans multiple industries, from chemicals to sports and beyond, and his influence stretches across continents.

With insight into his personal values, his business strategies, and his relentless drive to push boundaries, *Jim Ratcliffe: The Industrialist Behind INEOS* offers readers an in-depth look at one of the world's most enigmatic entrepreneurs, whose daring decisions have reshaped industries and cemented his legacy as a modern industrial titan.

Jim Ratcliffe

CHAPTER 1: WHO IS JIM RATCLIFFE

Jim Ratcliffe is a British billionaire and the founder, chairman, and CEO of *INEOS*, a multinational chemicals company. As one of the UK's richest individuals, Ratcliffe built his fortune by acquiring underperforming chemical plants and turning them into profitable ventures. He is known for his risk-taking approach to business, with INEOS becoming one of the world's largest chemical companies under his leadership.

Ratcliffe has a keen interest in sports and has expanded his business portfolio into this arena. He owns the *INEOS Grenadiers* cycling team, has invested in sailing through the *INEOS Team UK* in the America's Cup, and has stakes in football clubs such as *OGC Nice* in France and a minority stake in the *Mercedes-AMG Petronas Formula 1 Team*. Recently, he has also been involved in efforts to purchase a controlling stake in Manchester United Football Club.

Jim Ratcliffe

Apart from his business and sports interests, Ratcliffe is known for being a strong advocate for Brexit and has been involved in several high-profile philanthropic initiatives.

Early life and upbringing

Jim Ratcliffe was born on October 18, 1952, in Failsworth, a small town near Manchester, England. His early life was shaped by his working-class roots, and much of his success can be traced back to the values he learned during his formative years. His father was a joiner who later worked in a factory, while his mother was an office worker. This modest upbringing gave Ratcliffe a grounded perspective, and he developed a strong work ethic from an early age, understanding the value of hard work and perseverance.

Growing up in a post-war Britain that was still recovering economically, Ratcliffe's family did not have many luxuries, but they emphasized education and ambition. As a boy, he attended the local grammar school, where he showed an early aptitude for science and math.

Early Influences: Shaping the Industrialist Mindset

Jim Ratcliffe's journey into becoming one of the most influential industrialists of his time was shaped by a series of early experiences and influences that helped forge his distinctive mindset. Growing up in a working-class neighborhood in Manchester, Ratcliffe was surrounded by the gritty industrial landscape of northern England, a region renowned for its role in the Industrial Revolution. This environment, characterized by factories, manufacturing plants, and the working spirit of local communities, laid the groundwork for his fascination with industry and engineering.

Jim Ratcliffe

From a young age, Ratcliffe exhibited a curiosity about how things worked. His early life was marked by a practical, hands-on approach to learning, which complemented the industrial backdrop of Manchester. The area's rich history in textiles, chemicals, and manufacturing exposed him to the complexities of large-scale production and supply chains, even before he pursued formal education. The industrious spirit of the region, combined with the realities of post-war Britain, left a profound impact on Ratcliffe, giving him an understanding of both the opportunities and challenges inherent in building and running industrial operations.

At home, Ratcliffe was raised by a father who worked as a joiner and a mother who was a stay-at-home parent. Though not wealthy, his family instilled in him the importance of hard work, frugality, and ambition. Ratcliffe often credits his father for nurturing his practical skills, and his upbringing in a modest household made him aware of the value of resourcefulness, a trait that would later become key in his business ventures. The values of perseverance and self-reliance were deeply embedded in his character, helping him develop the mental resilience needed to tackle the risks and complexities of the business world.

Ratcliffe's education further shaped his industrialist mindset. He attended a local grammar school, where he excelled in science and mathematics. These subjects laid the foundation for his analytical approach to problem-solving and decision-making. His academic success propelled him to the University of Birmingham, where he studied chemical engineering. This period of his life marked a crucial turning point, as he immersed himself in the technical aspects of the industry. Chemical engineering, with its emphasis on process design, efficiency, and large-scale production, perfectly aligned with Ratcliffe's interest in creating and managing industrial systems. This technical knowledge would later become a key pillar in the growth of his empire, INEOS.

Beyond the classroom, Ratcliffe was influenced by the economic climate of Britain in the 1970s and 1980s. The country was undergoing significant industrial decline,

Jim Ratcliffe

with many traditional manufacturing sectors facing closures or downsizing. This environment of economic uncertainty and industrial transformation was crucial in shaping Ratcliffe's perspective on business. Rather than being deterred by the decline of Britain's industrial might, Ratcliffe saw opportunity. He recognized the potential for revitalizing struggling industries by improving efficiency and adopting innovative business practices. This foresight would guide him in acquiring underperforming assets and turning them into highly profitable ventures.

During his early career, Ratcliffe worked at companies like Esso and Courtaulds, where he gained firsthand experience in the operational and financial intricacies of large industrial firms. His time at Esso gave him exposure to the oil and petrochemical industries, where he began to understand the critical importance of raw materials and energy to industrial production. Courtaulds, a British chemical and textile manufacturer, provided him with insights into the challenges of running legacy businesses in a rapidly changing global market.

Jim Ratcliffe

These early professional experiences were instrumental in honing his ability to spot inefficiencies, cut costs, and make strategic acquisitions—key skills that would define his approach to building INEOS.

Ratcliffe's decision to pursue an MBA at the London Business School also had a profound impact on his mindset. The program exposed him to the world of finance, mergers, and acquisitions, broadening his understanding of how to leverage capital for industrial growth. It was here that Ratcliffe began to formulate the idea that would later become his hallmark: using debt to finance acquisitions and quickly turning those acquisitions into profitable ventures by streamlining operations and reducing costs. This financial acumen, combined with his technical background in chemical engineering, gave him a unique edge in the competitive world of industrial business.

In addition to formal education and professional experiences, Ratcliffe's personality played a significant role in shaping his industrialist mindset. He has often

Jim Ratcliffe

been described as determined, pragmatic, and highly focused. These traits enabled him to take bold risks, such as acquiring large and often struggling companies, while remaining grounded in the practical realities of running them efficiently. His willingness to embrace uncertainty, combined with a relentless drive for success, has been key to his ability to navigate the complex and often volatile industrial landscape.

Moreover, Ratcliffe's keen interest in sport and adventure, from marathon running to sailing, reflects his competitive nature and appetite for challenge. These personal interests mirror his business philosophy, where he consistently seeks out the most difficult challenges in industry and pushes boundaries to achieve success. This drive for excellence and a desire to outperform competitors is reflected in his approach to INEOS, where he consistently invests in cutting-edge technology and infrastructure to stay ahead of the competition.

In conclusion, Jim Ratcliffe's industrialist mindset was shaped by a confluence of early influences—his

Jim Ratcliffe

upbringing in industrial Manchester, the values instilled by his family, his education in chemical engineering, his exposure to the business world, and his personal determination to succeed. Together, these factors forged a powerful combination of technical expertise, financial savvy, and a fearless approach to business, setting the stage for his future success as the head of INEOS.

CHAPTER 2: THE PATH TO INDUSTRIAL SUCCESS

Jim Ratcliffe's path to industrial success is a story of ambition, strategic vision, and calculated risk-taking. From the very beginning of his career, Ratcliffe demonstrated a knack for identifying opportunities in complex, capital-intensive industries, and transforming them into highly profitable ventures. His journey, marked by key moments of decision and transition, began in the relatively modest world of engineering and finance before culminating in the creation of INEOS, one of the world's largest chemical companies.

After completing his degree in chemical engineering at the University of Birmingham, Ratcliffe entered the workforce at a time when Britain's industrial landscape was changing dramatically. His first significant role was at Esso, where he gained essential experience in the petrochemical industry. At Esso, he was exposed to the

Jim Ratcliffe

intricacies of energy, chemicals, and the supply chain dynamics that underpin large industrial operations. This period allowed him to observe firsthand the operational challenges that businesses in the chemical and energy sectors faced, such as the volatility of raw material prices and the complexities of large-scale production.

Although Esso gave him valuable technical experience, Ratcliffe's ambition led him to seek broader business knowledge. He soon moved to Courtaulds, a British multinational specializing in textiles and chemicals. At Courtaulds, he was involved in project management, which gave him a taste of leadership and responsibility. Here, Ratcliffe observed the difficulties of running a legacy company—one that had been successful in the past but was now grappling with the economic realities of a rapidly changing market. The experience reinforced his belief that even well-established companies could fail if they did not innovate or remain cost-effective.

Despite his technical background, Ratcliffe was keenly aware that success in modern industry required more

Jim Ratcliffe

than engineering expertise; it required financial acumen and a deep understanding of corporate strategy. This realization led him to pursue an MBA at the London Business School, a decision that would prove pivotal in his career. The program exposed Ratcliffe to a world of finance, capital markets, and mergers and acquisitions (M&A), all of which were relatively unfamiliar to him at the time. It was during his MBA studies that he began to understand the power of leveraged buyouts (LBOs)—the practice of using debt to acquire companies and restructuring them for profitability. This financial technique would later become central to his business model

The Management Consultant Years at Esso and Courtaulds

Jim Ratcliffe's years as a management consultant at Esso and Courtaulds were formative in shaping his understanding of the industrial world and the business strategies that would later define his success. These experiences allowed him to gain a deep insight into both the technical and operational aspects of large-scale industrial enterprises, while also exposing him to the financial and strategic elements of management.

At Esso, Ratcliffe was introduced to the energy and petrochemical industry, a sector that would play a significant role in his future ventures. Esso, a subsidiary of the global giant Exxon, was a leader in the oil and gas industry, providing Ratcliffe with exposure to the complexities of a multinational corporation. His role at Esso involved technical project management and operations, giving him hands-on experience with the production processes, supply chains, and logistics that are integral to the energy sector. He was responsible for ensuring that projects were delivered on time and within budget, which required a keen understanding of both the technical details and the broader business objectives.

This period at Esso also offered Ratcliffe his first exposure to the challenges of managing resources in a volatile market. The oil industry, subject to fluctuations in global supply and demand, taught him the importance of operational efficiency and cost control. These lessons in resource management and efficiency would become central themes in his later business ventures, particularly in the way he managed INEOS with its lean operational model and focus on profitability through cost reduction.

Ratcliffe's time at Esso was also a period of learning about corporate culture and the dynamics of large, bureaucratic organizations. While he gained valuable experience in managing large-scale industrial projects, he also became acutely aware of the limitations imposed by corporate hierarchies and slow decision-making processes.

MBA at London Business School: Building Strategic Acumen

Jim Ratcliffe

Jim Ratcliffe's decision to pursue an MBA at the London Business School was a transformative chapter in his journey toward becoming one of the world's most successful industrialists. By the time he entered the program, Ratcliffe had already accumulated valuable experience working in the chemical and energy sectors with Esso and Courtaulds. However, he recognized that to achieve his larger ambitions, he needed a deeper understanding of corporate finance, strategy, and entrepreneurship—skills that would allow him to move beyond technical roles into broader leadership positions. His time at London Business School played a crucial role in building this strategic acumen and equipping him with the tools to navigate the complex world of business and industry.

The MBA program provided Ratcliffe with a holistic view of business operations, stretching far beyond the technical aspects of industry that he had previously focused on. He immersed himself in subjects such as finance, mergers and acquisitions (M&A), corporate strategy, and leadership, all of which laid the groundwork for his future endeavors. One of the key benefits of the MBA program was that it exposed Ratcliffe to the world of high-level corporate decision-making and strategic planning. He began to see business not just as a technical or operational challenge but as a strategic endeavor that involved making bold decisions about capital allocation, risk management, and long-term growth.

Finance, in particular, became an area of deep interest for Ratcliffe. While he had previously been involved in managing projects and operations, his MBA introduced him to the intricacies of capital markets, investment strategies, and financial instruments. He learned how to assess companies' financial health, understand balance sheets, and analyze profitability, all of which would later prove invaluable in his approach to building INEOS. The concept of leveraged buyouts (LBOs)—where a company is acquired using a significant amount of borrowed money—was particularly fascinating to Ratcliffe. He understood that with the right financial strategy, underperforming or undervalued companies could be acquired and turned around for profit, using debt as a key tool for expansion. This financial approach would become a cornerstone of his business philosophy in the years to come.

Ratcliffe's time at London Business School also deepened his understanding of risk and reward in business. Through case studies and real-world examples, he saw how successful businesses had leveraged risks to their advantage, and he began to develop a keen sense of how to identify and manage risks effectively. This understanding would later give him the confidence to make bold, high-stakes decisions, such as acquiring major assets in the chemicals industry at times when others might have hesitated. His ability to assess risks and act decisively became one of his defining characteristics as a business leader.

Another key aspect of the MBA experience was the exposure to entrepreneurship and innovation. Ratcliffe had always been interested in the idea of building something from the ground up, and his studies at London

Jim Ratcliffe

Business School reinforced this ambition. He was able to analyze entrepreneurial ventures, understand market dynamics, and study how startups could disrupt traditional industries. This

Transition into Private Equity: A New Direction

Jim Ratcliffe's transition into private equity marked a pivotal moment in his career, setting the stage for the eventual creation of INEOS and defining his approach to business in the industrial sector. After completing his MBA at the London Business School, Ratcliffe recognized that the private equity space offered him the opportunity to leverage his technical expertise, strategic acumen, and entrepreneurial spirit in a way that traditional corporate roles could not. This shift was motivated by his desire to take on more significant challenges and exert greater control over business

Jim Ratcliffe

decisions, enabling him to pursue his vision for success in the industrial landscape.

Entering the private equity world was not merely a career change for Ratcliffe; it was a fundamental shift in his perspective on business. Private equity firms typically acquire companies, improve their operations, and then sell them for a profit within a defined period. This model resonated with Ratcliffe, as it combined his interests in engineering, finance, and corporate strategy. He saw an opportunity to apply the skills he had developed during his time at Esso and Courtaulds in a more dynamic and impactful way. Private equity allowed him to engage with underperforming companies, implement operational efficiencies, and drive growth, all while utilizing the financial techniques he had learned during his MBA.

During this transition, Ratcliffe gained invaluable experience working with various private equity firms, including the notable firm, **Harris Williams & Co.** His role involved evaluating potential acquisitions, assessing the financial health of target companies, and devising strategies for operational improvements. Ratcliffe quickly became adept at identifying undervalued assets with significant turnaround potential. He developed a keen eye for spotting opportunities in sectors that were either struggling or undergoing transformation, skills that would become central to his future successes.

This phase of Ratcliffe's career was characterized by a hands-on approach to management. He realized that the true value in private equity lay not only in financial engineering but also in the operational improvements that could be made post-acquisition. He began to implement strategies that focused on cost reduction, process optimization, and innovative business practices. By engaging directly with the management teams of the companies he worked with, he could influence their operational strategies and drive performance improvements. This proactive management style, which emphasized collaboration and shared vision, would later become a hallmark of his leadership at INEOS.

Jim Ratcliffe

Ratcliffe's exposure to various industries during his time in private equity further broadened his understanding of the business landscape. He encountered different operational models and management practices, learning to navigate the complexities of various sectors. This experience equipped him with the versatility and adaptability needed to thrive in the industrial arena. As he became more entrenched in the private equity world, he began to formulate his vision of building a company that could capitalize on the inefficiencies he had identified across the industries he engaged with.

One of the defining moments of Ratcliffe's transition into private equity came with his involvement in the acquisition of **Innovene**, a major player in the petrochemical industry. This opportunity represented a significant leap for Ratcliffe, allowing him to apply his accumulated knowledge and skills on a larger scale. Innovene was a subsidiary of BP, and at the time of its acquisition, it was struggling with inefficiencies and underperformance. Ratcliffe recognized the potential for

Jim Ratcliffe

transformation and leveraged his experience to turn Innovene into a more competitive entity.

The acquisition of Innovene was instrumental not just in Ratcliffe's career but also in shaping the foundation for INEOS. It was during this process that he began to understand the full potential of the chemicals industry and the role that strategic acquisitions could play in building a substantial business. He demonstrated a unique ability to assess the potential for operational improvements, streamline processes, and create value in a way that few others in the industry were doing at the time. Ratcliffe's success with Innovene solidified his reputation as a savvy industrialist and laid the groundwork for the subsequent formation of INEOS.

The experience also reinforced Ratcliffe's belief in the importance of a hands-on, operationally focused approach to leadership. He became known for his willingness to dive deep into the workings of the companies he acquired, often spending significant time on the ground with teams to understand their challenges

Jim Ratcliffe

and identify areas for improvement. This practical approach helped him foster a culture of accountability and performance, which would later become a cornerstone of INEOS's operational philosophy.

As he transitioned fully into private equity, Ratcliffe also began to develop a network of contacts and relationships within the industry that would prove invaluable. He understood that success in this arena relied not only on individual skills but also on building strategic partnerships and alliances. These connections would later facilitate his ability to raise capital, negotiate deals, and access resources that would support his ambitious plans for growth.

Ultimately, Ratcliffe's transition into private equity was a decisive step that enabled him to marry his technical background with financial acumen and strategic vision. This phase of his career not only equipped him with the tools and experiences needed to launch INEOS but also instilled in him a mindset that embraced risk, innovation, and operational excellence. His ability to identify opportunities, implement effective strategies, and drive performance would serve as the bedrock of his approach to building one of the world's leading chemical companies. The lessons learned during this pivotal period laid the groundwork for Ratcliffe's enduring legacy in the industrial sector.

Jim Ratcliffe

CHAPTER 3: FOUNDING INEOS

The founding of INEOS was a defining moment in Jim Ratcliffe's career, marking the culmination of years of experience in the chemical and energy sectors, as well as his strategic vision for creating a new kind of industrial company. Following his successful stint in private equity and the transformational acquisition of Innovene, Ratcliffe saw an opportunity to create a global leader in the chemicals industry. His ambition was to build a company that not only excelled in operational efficiency but also prioritized innovation, sustainability, and adaptability in an ever-evolving market.

In 1998, Ratcliffe took a bold step by acquiring the Innovene business from BP, which included several large-scale manufacturing plants and a diverse portfolio of chemical products. This acquisition laid the foundation for what would become INEOS. At the time, Innovene was struggling, having faced significant operational challenges and underperformance. However,

Jim Ratcliffe

Ratcliffe recognized its potential and saw it as a platform to build a new enterprise. His vision was not merely to revitalize Innovene but to create a company that could compete on a global scale in the chemicals market.

From the outset, Ratcliffe's approach to founding INEOS was characterized by a focus on operational excellence. He believed that by streamlining processes and improving efficiencies, he could create significant value not just for the company but also for its customers and stakeholders. He implemented rigorous performance metrics and accountability measures across the organization, ensuring that every aspect of the operation was optimized for success. This hands-on leadership style enabled Ratcliffe to engage directly with employees and instill a culture of performance and continuous improvement.

Ratcliffe also understood the importance of investing in technology and innovation. Under his leadership, INEOS made significant investments in research and development to create new products and improve

Jim Ratcliffe

existing ones. Ratcliffe believed that staying ahead of the competition required a commitment to innovation, particularly in the chemical sector, where advancements could lead to more sustainable practices and enhanced product offerings. This focus on R&D became a core principle of INEOS, differentiating it from many traditional players in the industry.

Another key aspect of Ratcliffe's strategy in founding INEOS was his emphasis on sustainability. As environmental concerns became increasingly prominent in the global conversation, Ratcliffe recognized the need for the chemicals industry to adapt and evolve. He positioned INEOS as a forward-thinking company that would take responsibility for its environmental impact while still delivering high-quality products. This commitment to sustainability resonated with customers and investors alike, enhancing the company's reputation and solidifying its place in the market.

Financially, Ratcliffe employed a unique model that involved leveraging debt to finance growth. This approach, honed during his years in private equity, allowed INEOS to make strategic acquisitions and expand rapidly without sacrificing operational control. Ratcliffe was willing to take calculated risks, understanding that the potential for high returns often required an upfront investment. This financial strategy proved effective, enabling INEOS to acquire several key assets in the chemicals sector and rapidly grow its market presence.

As INEOS grew, Ratcliffe's leadership style and vision attracted top talent from within the industry. He focused on creating a collaborative and performance-driven culture, empowering employees to contribute ideas and solutions. Ratcliffe believed in building teams that were not only skilled but also aligned with the company's vision and values. This commitment to talent development helped foster a strong organizational culture that emphasized accountability, innovation, and a shared commitment to excellence.

Jim Ratcliffe

The company's growth trajectory was further accelerated by Ratcliffe's willingness to enter emerging markets. Recognizing the potential for expansion beyond Europe, INEOS began to explore opportunities in North America and Asia. Ratcliffe understood that to establish INEOS as a global leader, it was essential to tap into the rapidly growing markets in these regions. This foresight led to the establishment of key production facilities

Acquiring the BP Chemicals Division: A Game-Changer

Acquiring the BP Chemicals Division was a pivotal moment in Jim Ratcliffe's career and the trajectory of INEOS, representing a bold and strategic move that would significantly alter the landscape of the global chemicals industry. The deal, finalized in 2005, was not merely an expansion for INEOS; it was a transformative acquisition that positioned the company as a major player in the sector and established Ratcliffe's reputation as a savvy industrialist.

The BP Chemicals Division was a substantial asset within the BP conglomerate, encompassing a diverse range of chemical products and manufacturing facilities. At the time of the acquisition, BP was undergoing restructuring and reevaluating its portfolio, leading to the decision to divest non-core assets, including its chemicals division. Recognizing an opportunity, Ratcliffe saw the potential to acquire a well-established business that was, at that time, undervalued and facing operational challenges. He understood that with the right management and strategic direction, he could turn the division around and unlock significant value.

The acquisition was characterized by its scale and complexity. Ratcliffe and his team meticulously analyzed BP Chemicals' operations, identifying inefficiencies and areas for improvement. The division's portfolio included key products such as polyethylene and polypropylene, which were essential to various industries, including

Jim Ratcliffe

packaging, automotive, and construction. Ratcliffe recognized that these products were in high demand and that with a strategic overhaul, the division could become a highly profitable segment of INEOS.

Securing the necessary financing for the acquisition was a testament to Ratcliffe's skills in private equity. He expertly navigated the financial landscape, leveraging the company's existing assets and relationships to arrange the capital required for the deal. The transaction was substantial, amounting to approximately $9 billion, which underscored Ratcliffe's willingness to take calculated risks in pursuit of growth. This ability to manage debt effectively, coupled with a focus on operational improvements, would later prove crucial in INEOS's success post-acquisition.

Once the acquisition was complete, Ratcliffe implemented a comprehensive strategy to integrate BP Chemicals into INEOS. He initiated a thorough evaluation of the division's operations, focusing on streamlining processes, reducing costs, and enhancing

Jim Ratcliffe

production efficiency. Ratcliffe's hands-on management style came to the forefront during this phase as he engaged directly with employees and leadership teams to foster a culture of accountability and performance. He encouraged innovation and operational excellence, making it clear that he expected significant improvements in productivity and profitability.

One of the key challenges Ratcliffe faced was revitalizing the workforce and addressing the organizational culture that had developed within BP Chemicals. He recognized that to unlock the full potential of the acquired division, it was essential to motivate employees and align them with INEOS's vision and values. Ratcliffe prioritized open communication and collaboration, creating an environment where employees felt empowered to contribute their ideas and insights. This approach not only helped to improve morale but also led to enhanced operational performance.

Jim Ratcliffe

In the wake of the acquisition, INEOS quickly began to see positive results. The integration of BP Chemicals significantly expanded the company's production capacity and product portfolio, allowing it to meet growing demand in key markets. Ratcliffe's focus on operational efficiency and cost management yielded impressive financial returns, enabling INEOS to strengthen its position in the competitive chemicals sector. The success of the acquisition reaffirmed Ratcliffe's belief in the potential of strategic acquisitions as a means of driving growth and enhancing shareholder value.

Moreover, the acquisition of BP Chemicals also positioned INEOS as a leader in sustainability initiatives within the chemicals industry. Ratcliffe recognized the importance of addressing environmental concerns and was committed to reducing the environmental impact of the acquired operations. He implemented measures aimed at improving energy efficiency and reducing emissions, aligning INEOS with the growing emphasis on sustainability in the global market. This forward-thinking approach not only appealed to environmentally conscious consumers but also attracted investors looking for companies that prioritized sustainable practices.

In the years following the acquisition, INEOS experienced exponential growth, solidifying its reputation as one of the largest and most successful chemical companies in the world. Ratcliffe's vision and strategic foresight in acquiring the BP Chemicals Division proved to be a game-changer for both the company and his career. The deal showcased his ability to identify opportunities in the market, navigate complex acquisitions, and drive operational excellence—all hallmarks of his leadership style.

Overall, acquiring the BP Chemicals Division was a watershed moment for Jim Ratcliffe and INEOS. It not only expanded the company's capabilities and market presence but also laid the groundwork for future growth and innovation. Ratcliffe's hands-on leadership, strategic vision, and commitment to operational excellence turned

Jim Ratcliffe

the division into a critical component of INEOS's success, propelling the company to new heights and cementing Ratcliffe's legacy as a transformative figure in the chemicals industry.

INEOS' Growth Strategy: A Focus on Cost Efficiency and M&A

Jim Ratcliffe's leadership of INEOS has been characterized by a dynamic growth strategy that emphasizes cost efficiency and strategic mergers and acquisitions (M&A). This dual approach has played a pivotal role in transforming INEOS into one of the world's leading chemical companies. Ratcliffe's vision has always been to build a resilient organization capable of adapting to market fluctuations while consistently delivering value to stakeholders. By focusing on operational efficiency and pursuing targeted acquisitions, Ratcliffe has established a model for sustainable growth that has set INEOS apart from its competitors.

Jim Ratcliffe

Cost efficiency has been a cornerstone of INEOS's growth strategy. From the outset, Ratcliffe understood that to compete effectively in the global chemicals market, the company needed to operate at the highest levels of efficiency. He implemented rigorous performance metrics and continuous improvement programs aimed at streamlining operations across all facilities. This included everything from optimizing production processes to reducing waste and minimizing energy consumption. By fostering a culture of efficiency, Ratcliffe encouraged employees at all levels to identify areas for improvement and contribute to operational excellence.

One of the key methods Ratcliffe employed to enhance cost efficiency was the adoption of best practices from various industries. He believed that the chemicals sector could learn a great deal from other fields, particularly in terms of operational management and technology adoption. Ratcliffe encouraged cross-industry collaboration and knowledge sharing, allowing INEOS

Jim Ratcliffe

to implement innovative practices that led to significant cost savings. This proactive approach not only improved profitability but also positioned INEOS as a forward-thinking leader in the industry.

Ratcliffe's commitment to cost efficiency extended to the company's supply chain management. He recognized that optimizing logistics and procurement processes could have a profound impact on overall operational costs. By negotiating favorable contracts with suppliers and investing in state-of-the-art logistics systems, INEOS was able to reduce costs while ensuring the timely delivery of raw materials and products. This focus on supply chain efficiency not only improved margins but also enhanced the company's ability to respond quickly to changing market demands.

In addition to enhancing cost efficiency, Ratcliffe placed a significant emphasis on strategic M&A as a means of accelerating INEOS's growth. He believed that acquiring companies with complementary strengths could provide a pathway to rapid expansion and diversification. By

Jim Ratcliffe

carefully selecting targets that aligned with INEOS's core competencies, Ratcliffe was able to leverage existing resources and expertise to maximize the potential of acquired businesses.

Ratcliffe's approach to M&A was characterized by meticulous due diligence and a clear focus on integration. He understood that the success of an acquisition depended not only on the financials but also on how well the two organizations could work together post-acquisition. Ratcliffe was hands-on during the integration process, often immersing himself in the operations of newly acquired companies to ensure alignment with INEOS's strategic vision. This level of engagement helped to facilitate smoother transitions and foster a culture of collaboration, enabling INEOS to extract maximum value from each acquisition.

Under Ratcliffe's leadership, INEOS pursued a series of high-profile acquisitions that significantly expanded its capabilities and market presence. These deals were not just about growth for growth's sake; each acquisition

Jim Ratcliffe

was strategically aligned with INEOS's long-term goals. For instance, the acquisition of BP Chemicals provided INEOS with a robust product portfolio and increased production capacity, while the purchase of other businesses in the petrochemical sector allowed the company to diversify its offerings and enter new markets. This strategic focus on M&A ensured that INEOS not only grew in size but also enhanced its competitive position within the industry.

Ratcliffe also recognized the importance of innovation in driving growth and maintaining a competitive edge. He championed research and development initiatives, encouraging teams to explore new technologies and develop innovative products that could meet the evolving needs of customers. By fostering a culture of innovation, Ratcliffe positioned INEOS as a leader in sustainable solutions within the chemicals sector. This forward-looking approach attracted new customers and markets, contributing to the company's overall growth strategy.

Jim Ratcliffe

The combination of cost efficiency and strategic M&A has proven to be a winning formula for INEOS. Ratcliffe's leadership has resulted in impressive financial performance, with the company consistently delivering strong profits and shareholder returns. This financial success has provided INEOS with the resources needed to continue its growth trajectory, reinvesting in operations, pursuing new acquisitions, and expanding into emerging markets.

Furthermore, Ratcliffe's focus on sustainability has become an integral part of INEOS's growth strategy. Recognizing the increasing importance of environmental responsibility in the chemicals industry, he has made significant investments in sustainable practices and technologies. This commitment not only enhances INEOS's reputation but also opens up new opportunities in markets where customers are increasingly prioritizing sustainability in their purchasing decisions.

In summary, Jim Ratcliffe's growth strategy for INEOS revolves around a relentless focus on cost efficiency and strategic mergers and acquisitions. This dual approach has allowed INEOS to achieve remarkable growth, positioning it as a global leader in the chemicals sector. By instilling a culture of operational excellence, fostering innovation, and pursuing targeted acquisitions, Ratcliffe has successfully transformed INEOS into a resilient organization capable of navigating the complexities of the global market. As INEOS continues to evolve, Ratcliffe's vision and strategic leadership remain at the forefront of its ongoing success.

The INEOS Business Model: Lean Operations, Bold Acquisitions

The INEOS business model, under Jim Ratcliffe's leadership, is defined by its emphasis on lean operations and bold acquisitions, a combination that has enabled the company to thrive in the highly competitive chemicals industry. This strategic framework not only positions INEOS as a leader in operational efficiency but also as a formidable player in the global market through calculated expansion.

At the heart of the INEOS business model is the principle of lean operations. Ratcliffe has instilled a culture of efficiency and productivity throughout the organization, encouraging all employees to identify and eliminate waste in processes. This approach stems from his belief that in a sector where margins can be tight, operating with minimal waste is essential for sustaining profitability. INEOS employs various lean methodologies to streamline its manufacturing processes, reduce cycle times, and optimize resource allocation. By focusing on continuous improvement, the company enhances its ability to respond to market demands swiftly and effectively.

Central to INEOS's lean operations is its commitment to operational excellence. The company rigorously tracks performance metrics and key performance indicators (KPIs), allowing it to identify inefficiencies and implement corrective actions quickly. Ratcliffe

Jim Ratcliffe

emphasizes the importance of data-driven decision-making, ensuring that managers at all levels have access to real-time performance data. This transparency fosters accountability and encourages a proactive approach to problem-solving, ultimately leading to improved operational outcomes.

Furthermore, INEOS invests in advanced technologies and automation to enhance its operational capabilities. By adopting cutting-edge manufacturing technologies, the company can increase productivity and reduce costs. Ratcliffe recognizes that technological advancements can significantly improve efficiency, and he has prioritized investments in automation and digital solutions. This forward-thinking approach not only enhances operational capabilities but also positions INEOS as a leader in innovation within the chemicals sector.

Another critical aspect of the INEOS business model is its approach to acquisitions. Ratcliffe is known for his bold and strategic mindset when it comes to pursuing opportunities for growth through M&A. He believes that

Jim Ratcliffe

acquiring companies with complementary strengths can accelerate INEOS's expansion and diversification. This approach has been instrumental in the company's growth trajectory, enabling it to expand its product offerings, enter new markets, and enhance its competitive position.

When Ratcliffe identifies potential acquisition targets, he conducts meticulous due diligence to assess their operational performance, market position, and cultural fit with INEOS. This thorough analysis ensures that each acquisition aligns with the company's long-term strategic goals. Ratcliffe's experience in private equity has provided him with the skills necessary to evaluate the financial aspects of potential deals, allowing him to negotiate favorable terms and structure acquisitions that maximize value for INEOS.

Once an acquisition is completed, Ratcliffe takes a hands-on approach to integration. He believes that the success of an acquisition hinges not only on the initial purchase but also on how well the new entity is integrated into INEOS's existing operations. Ratcliffe

Jim Ratcliffe

emphasizes the importance of aligning cultures, processes, and systems to create a unified organization. By fostering collaboration and open communication between teams, he ensures that the strengths of the acquired company are leveraged while maintaining the operational efficiency that defines INEOS.

In addition to enhancing operational efficiency and pursuing acquisitions, INEOS's business model is characterized by its commitment to sustainability. Ratcliffe recognizes that environmental responsibility is increasingly important in the chemicals industry, and he has made it a priority to integrate sustainable practices into the company's operations. This includes investing in technologies that reduce emissions, improve energy efficiency, and promote recycling and waste reduction. By prioritizing sustainability, INEOS not only addresses regulatory and consumer demands but also positions itself favorably in a market where customers are seeking environmentally responsible solutions.

Jim Ratcliffe

The synergy between lean operations and bold acquisitions creates a powerful business model that has enabled INEOS to achieve impressive growth. By continuously improving operational efficiency, the company can maintain competitive pricing while delivering high-quality products. Simultaneously, the strategic acquisitions expand INEOS's market presence and enhance its product portfolio, creating opportunities for cross-selling and synergies between different business units.

Ratcliffe's leadership has been instrumental in driving the success of the INEOS business model. His focus on creating a performance-driven culture, fostering innovation, and pursuing strategic growth has transformed INEOS into a globally recognized leader in the chemicals sector. As the company continues to evolve, Ratcliffe's commitment to lean operations and bold acquisitions will remain central to its ongoing success.

Jim Ratcliffe

In summary, the INEOS business model is built on the foundations of lean operations and bold acquisitions. This dual approach allows the company to operate efficiently while strategically expanding its capabilities and market presence. By prioritizing operational excellence, investing in technology, and pursuing targeted acquisitions, INEOS has positioned itself for sustained growth and success in the competitive chemicals industry. Jim Ratcliffe's vision and leadership are key drivers of this innovative business model, ensuring that INEOS remains at the forefront of the global market.

Jim Ratcliffe

CHAPTER 4: EXPANDING THE EMPIRE

Expanding the empire of INEOS has been a central focus of Jim Ratcliffe's strategic vision since he founded the company in 1998. This ambition to grow and diversify the company has led to significant milestones and developments that have solidified INEOS's position as a global leader in the chemicals industry. Ratcliffe's approach to expansion combines strategic acquisitions, investments in new technologies, and a commitment to sustainability, resulting in a multifaceted growth strategy that continues to evolve.

One of the defining aspects of INEOS's expansion has been its aggressive pursuit of acquisitions. Ratcliffe has strategically identified and acquired companies that complement INEOS's core capabilities, enabling the firm to broaden its product offerings and enter new markets. For example, the acquisition of BP Chemicals in 2005 was a significant milestone that dramatically increased INEOS's production capacity and market share. This acquisition not only expanded the company's product portfolio to include a diverse range of petrochemical products but also strengthened its operational infrastructure, allowing for enhanced efficiencies and cost savings.

In the years following the acquisition of BP Chemicals, Ratcliffe continued to seek out opportunities for growth through M&A. The acquisition of Styrolution in 2016 was another critical step in expanding INEOS's footprint in the global chemicals market. By integrating Styrolution's expertise in styrenics, INEOS not only diversified its product line but also established a strong presence in high-demand sectors such as automotive, construction, and consumer goods. This strategic acquisition underscored Ratcliffe's vision of creating a well-rounded and resilient business capable of adapting to market fluctuations.

Beyond traditional acquisitions, Ratcliffe has also explored joint ventures and partnerships as a means of expanding INEOS's capabilities. By collaborating with

Jim Ratcliffe

other industry leaders, INEOS has been able to leverage shared expertise and resources, enabling the company to accelerate its growth while minimizing risks associated with entering new markets. These strategic alliances have facilitated the development of innovative products and technologies, further enhancing INEOS's competitive position.

The expansion of INEOS has not been limited to acquisitions; Ratcliffe has also prioritized investments in new facilities and technologies. He recognized the importance of keeping pace with industry advancements and evolving customer needs. As part of this strategy, INEOS has invested heavily in state-of-the-art manufacturing plants and R&D facilities. For instance, the establishment of the INEOS Innovation Centre in London demonstrates Ratcliffe's commitment to driving innovation within the company. This facility serves as a hub for research and development, enabling INEOS to create new products and processes that meet the demands of a rapidly changing market.

Jim Ratcliffe

Sustainability has become an increasingly important component of INEOS's expansion strategy. Ratcliffe understands that environmental responsibility is essential for long-term growth and success in the chemicals industry. As such, he has led initiatives aimed at reducing the company's environmental footprint and promoting sustainable practices. For example, INEOS has invested in technologies that enhance energy efficiency, reduce greenhouse gas emissions, and promote recycling initiatives. By integrating sustainability into its core operations, INEOS not only meets regulatory requirements but also aligns with the growing consumer demand for environmentally responsible products.

The expansion of INEOS's operations has also involved a geographical diversification strategy. Ratcliffe has pursued growth opportunities beyond traditional markets in Europe and North America, seeking to establish a presence in emerging markets. For instance, INEOS has made significant inroads into the Asian market, recognizing the region's increasing demand for

Jim Ratcliffe

chemicals and materials. This geographic expansion has positioned INEOS to capture new customer bases and capitalize on the growth potential of developing economies.

In addition to geographical expansion, Ratcliffe has also focused on diversifying the company's product offerings. By investing in the development of innovative solutions, INEOS has expanded its reach into high-growth sectors such as renewable energy, electric vehicles, and advanced materials. This diversification not only mitigates risks associated with reliance on specific markets but also positions INEOS as a forward-thinking leader in emerging industries.

Ratcliffe's leadership style has played a crucial role in the successful expansion of INEOS. He is known for his hands-on approach and willingness to take calculated risks. This mindset has allowed him to make bold decisions that propel the company forward. Ratcliffe's ability to identify opportunities and capitalize on them quickly has been instrumental in INEOS's growth

Jim Ratcliffe

trajectory, as evidenced by the company's impressive financial performance and market presence.

Furthermore, Ratcliffe has fostered a culture of innovation within INEOS, encouraging employees to think creatively and challenge the status quo. This emphasis on innovation has resulted in the development of new products and processes that meet the changing needs of customers, enhancing INEOS's competitive edge in the market. By empowering employees to contribute ideas and solutions, Ratcliffe has cultivated an environment where innovation thrives.

In summary, the expansion of INEOS under Jim Ratcliffe's leadership has been driven by a combination of strategic acquisitions, investments in new technologies, a commitment to sustainability, and a focus on geographic and product diversification. This multifaceted approach has allowed INEOS to solidify its position as a global leader in the chemicals industry while continually adapting to market changes and customer demands. Ratcliffe's visionary leadership,

Jim Ratcliffe

coupled with a culture of innovation and a willingness to embrace new opportunities, has set the stage for continued growth and success for INEOS in the years to come.

Global Expansion: INEOS' Operations in Europe, Asia, and America

Jim Ratcliffe's strategic vision for INEOS has driven the company's global expansion, establishing it as a significant player in the chemicals industry across Europe, Asia, and America. This broad international presence reflects Ratcliffe's commitment to capturing growth opportunities and responding to the diverse demands of global markets. The expansion into these regions has not only increased INEOS's production capabilities but also enhanced its competitiveness and market reach.

Jim Ratcliffe

In Europe, INEOS has a well-established footprint, with numerous manufacturing plants and facilities strategically located across the continent. The company's operations span various countries, including the United Kingdom, Germany, France, and Belgium, where it has become one of the largest chemical producers. INEOS's European operations are characterized by their diverse product offerings, ranging from petrochemicals to specialty chemicals, serving a wide range of industries such as automotive, construction, and consumer goods.

The company's growth in Europe has been fueled by strategic acquisitions and investments in state-of-the-art manufacturing facilities. For example, the acquisition of BP Chemicals significantly enhanced INEOS's operational capabilities in Europe, allowing the company to expand its product portfolio and improve economies of scale. Ratcliffe's emphasis on operational efficiency has enabled INEOS to maintain competitive pricing while delivering high-quality products to its customers.

Jim Ratcliffe

Furthermore, INEOS has actively invested in research and development initiatives in Europe, focusing on innovation and sustainability. The establishment of the INEOS Innovation Centre in London serves as a hub for developing new technologies and products tailored to meet the evolving needs of European customers. This commitment to innovation ensures that INEOS remains at the forefront of the industry, addressing challenges such as environmental regulations and market shifts.

In Asia, Ratcliffe has recognized the region's growing demand for chemicals and materials, prompting INEOS to expand its operations significantly. The company has made strategic investments in several Asian countries, including China and Singapore, where it has established manufacturing facilities to serve local markets. By tapping into the burgeoning demand in Asia, INEOS aims to capture new customer bases and capitalize on the growth potential of the region's rapidly developing economies.

Jim Ratcliffe

INEOS's expansion into Asia has been marked by partnerships and joint ventures that enhance its market presence. Collaborating with local companies allows INEOS to leverage regional expertise and navigate the complexities of the Asian market effectively. These partnerships have facilitated access to new technologies, distribution networks, and customer relationships, positioning INEOS to capitalize on the diverse opportunities presented by the region's dynamic markets.

Moreover, INEOS has adapted its product offerings to meet the specific needs of Asian customers. By developing tailored solutions that address local preferences and regulatory requirements, the company has enhanced its competitiveness in the region. This customer-centric approach has resulted in increased sales and market share, further solidifying INEOS's position as a leading chemical producer in Asia.

In North America, INEOS has also made significant strides in expanding its operations. The company has invested heavily in the U.S. market, recognizing its potential as a major hub for chemical production. By establishing manufacturing plants in key locations, INEOS has positioned itself to serve various industries, including automotive, aerospace, and agriculture. The company's investments in North America are driven by the region's abundant resources and favorable business environment, including access to shale gas, which has lowered production costs for chemical manufacturers.

INEOS's strategic acquisitions in North America have further bolstered its growth in the region. By acquiring established companies with strong market positions, INEOS has quickly expanded its product offerings and customer base. This approach not only enhances INEOS's competitiveness but also allows the company to leverage existing distribution channels and customer relationships.

In addition to expanding its operational footprint, INEOS has prioritized sustainability in its North American operations. Recognizing the increasing importance of environmental responsibility in the chemical industry, the company has invested in technologies that promote energy efficiency and reduce emissions. This commitment to sustainability aligns with growing regulatory requirements and customer expectations, further enhancing INEOS's reputation in the market.

Throughout its global expansion, INEOS has maintained a strong focus on operational efficiency and innovation. Ratcliffe's leadership has fostered a culture that encourages employees to seek continuous improvement and embrace new technologies. This emphasis on operational excellence has allowed INEOS to respond swiftly to market changes and customer demands, ensuring its competitiveness in an ever-evolving industry.

Moreover, INEOS's global expansion strategy is supported by a robust supply chain network that facilitates efficient distribution and logistics. By optimizing its supply chain operations, the company can minimize costs and improve service levels to customers worldwide. This operational agility is essential in

Jim Ratcliffe

meeting the diverse needs of INEOS's global customer base and ensuring timely delivery of products.

In summary, Jim Ratcliffe's vision for global expansion has positioned INEOS as a leading player in the chemicals industry across Europe, Asia, and America. By strategically investing in manufacturing facilities, pursuing acquisitions, and fostering innovation, INEOS has successfully captured growth opportunities in diverse markets. Ratcliffe's commitment to operational efficiency and sustainability further enhances the company's competitiveness and reputation. As INEOS continues to expand its global footprint, its ability to adapt to local market conditions and customer demands will remain key to its ongoing success.

The Ongoing Push for Growth: Major Projects and Ventures

Jim Ratcliffe

Jim Ratcliffe's leadership at INEOS has been characterized by an unwavering commitment to growth, reflected in a series of major projects and ventures that have positioned the company as a formidable player in the global chemicals industry. Under his guidance, INEOS has embarked on ambitious initiatives that not only enhance its operational capabilities but also expand its market reach and product offerings. This ongoing push for growth is evident in several key projects that underscore Ratcliffe's vision for the future of the company.

One of the most notable projects in recent years has been INEOS's investment in the development of a new ethane cracker in the United States. This state-of-the-art facility is strategically located in Texas, where access to abundant natural gas resources provides a competitive advantage in feedstock costs. The ethane cracker is designed to produce ethylene, a critical building block for various chemicals and plastics, thereby enhancing INEOS's production capacity in North America. This major project not only solidifies INEOS's presence in the

Jim Ratcliffe

U.S. market but also aligns with Ratcliffe's strategy of capitalizing on the shale gas boom that has transformed the energy landscape in the region.

Strategic Partnerships and Joint Ventures in the Chemical Industry

Jim Ratcliffe's vision for INEOS has been significantly shaped by his approach to strategic partnerships and joint ventures within the chemical industry. Recognizing that collaboration can enhance competitiveness, foster innovation, and mitigate risks, Ratcliffe has actively pursued alliances that align with INEOS's strategic objectives. These partnerships have allowed the company to leverage complementary strengths, access new markets, and enhance its technological capabilities, positioning INEOS as a global leader in the chemicals sector.

Jim Ratcliffe

One of the hallmarks of Ratcliffe's strategy is his focus on forming partnerships that drive innovation and accelerate growth. For example, INEOS has engaged in joint ventures with leading players in the industry to develop advanced materials and technologies. Collaborating with firms that have specialized expertise allows INEOS to enhance its product offerings and respond more effectively to the evolving needs of customers. By pooling resources and knowledge, these partnerships have led to the creation of innovative solutions that address market demands while reducing development costs and timelines.

A notable example of such a partnership is the joint venture between INEOS and the French company Solvay to create INEOS Styrolution, a leading global supplier of styrenic plastics. This joint venture has enabled INEOS to capitalize on the growing demand for high-performance plastics used in automotive, construction, and consumer goods applications. By combining INEOS's extensive manufacturing capabilities with Solvay's expertise in specialty polymers, the joint venture has allowed both companies to strengthen their market positions and enhance their competitive advantage. This strategic collaboration exemplifies Ratcliffe's understanding of the importance of partnerships in driving growth and innovation.

In addition to joint ventures, Ratcliffe has also explored strategic alliances that facilitate access to new markets and customer bases. For instance, INEOS has formed partnerships with regional players in emerging markets, allowing the company to navigate local regulations and cultural nuances effectively. These alliances enable INEOS to tap into new growth opportunities while mitigating the risks associated with entering unfamiliar markets. By leveraging the local knowledge and networks of partners, INEOS can accelerate its expansion efforts and enhance its market penetration.

Ratcliffe's focus on sustainability has also influenced INEOS's approach to partnerships. In an era where environmental responsibility is paramount, collaborating with companies that prioritize sustainability can create synergies that enhance both parties' reputations and market positioning. INEOS has engaged in partnerships aimed at developing sustainable solutions, such as advanced recycling technologies that minimize waste and reduce the environmental impact of chemical production. These initiatives not only align with INEOS's sustainability goals but also resonate with the increasing demand for environmentally friendly products among consumers and businesses alike.

Moreover, Ratcliffe has recognized the importance of partnerships in advancing research and development initiatives. By collaborating with universities and research institutions, INEOS has access to cutting-edge technologies and scientific expertise that can drive innovation. These collaborations facilitate the development of new materials and processes that enhance the company's competitiveness in the market. For example, partnerships with academic institutions have led to breakthroughs in areas such as lightweight materials and advanced composites, positioning INEOS

Jim Ratcliffe

at the forefront of technological advancements in the chemical industry.

The strategic partnerships and joint ventures formed under Ratcliffe's leadership have not only contributed to INEOS's growth but also fostered a culture of collaboration within the organization. By encouraging employees to work closely with external partners, INEOS has created an environment that values knowledge sharing and innovation. This collaborative spirit has enabled the company to adapt to changing market conditions and continuously improve its offerings, ensuring its relevance in a competitive industry.

Furthermore, these strategic alliances have enhanced INEOS's resilience in the face of economic fluctuations and market uncertainties. By diversifying its partnerships and collaborating with various stakeholders, INEOS can mitigate risks associated with reliance on specific markets or technologies. This adaptability is particularly important in the chemicals industry, where demand can

Jim Ratcliffe

be influenced by factors such as geopolitical events, regulatory changes, and shifts in consumer preferences.

In conclusion, Jim Ratcliffe's emphasis on strategic partnerships and joint ventures has been instrumental in shaping the trajectory of INEOS. Through collaborations with industry leaders, regional players, and research institutions, INEOS has enhanced its innovation capabilities, expanded its market reach, and positioned itself as a leader in the global chemicals sector. Ratcliffe's understanding of the value of collaboration has fostered a culture of partnership within the organization, enabling INEOS to navigate challenges and seize growth opportunities in an ever-evolving industry. As the company continues to pursue strategic alliances, it remains well-equipped to thrive in the competitive landscape of the chemicals industry, driven by innovation and a commitment to sustainability.

Jim Ratcliffe

CHAPTER 5: INNOVATING IN ENERGY AND BEYOND

Under Jim Ratcliffe's leadership, INEOS has emerged as a prominent force in innovation, particularly in the energy sector and beyond. Ratcliffe's commitment to advancing technologies and processes has not only positioned INEOS as a leader in the chemical industry but also played a vital role in addressing some of the pressing challenges facing global energy markets today. His approach to innovation encompasses various aspects, including sustainability, efficiency, and the development of new materials and technologies that meet the demands of a rapidly changing world.

A cornerstone of INEOS's innovation strategy has been its focus on sustainability, especially in the energy sector. Ratcliffe recognizes that the traditional fossil fuel-based model is increasingly being challenged by the need for cleaner and more sustainable energy solutions. As a result, INEOS has invested heavily in research and development initiatives aimed at creating more sustainable alternatives. This includes exploring renewable energy sources, carbon capture technologies, and advanced recycling processes. By prioritizing sustainability, INEOS aims to reduce its environmental impact while continuing to provide essential products and services to its customers.

One notable initiative is INEOS's involvement in hydrogen production. Recognizing hydrogen as a key component of the future energy landscape, Ratcliffe has spearheaded efforts to develop technologies that facilitate the production and utilization of hydrogen as a clean energy source. INEOS is actively working on projects that leverage hydrogen's potential in various applications, including transportation and industrial processes. By investing in hydrogen technology, INEOS not only positions itself at the forefront of the energy transition but also contributes to reducing carbon emissions across multiple sectors.

Jim Ratcliffe

Moreover, INEOS has explored the potential of bio-based feedstocks as an alternative to traditional petrochemical processes. By investing in the development of biofuels and bio-based chemicals, Ratcliffe aims to diversify INEOS's product offerings while aligning with global trends toward sustainability. This innovation not only addresses consumer demand for greener products but also enhances the company's long-term viability in a world increasingly focused on reducing reliance on fossil fuels. The company's investments in biotechnology and research partnerships with academic institutions exemplify its commitment to advancing bio-based solutions that can transform the chemical industry.

In addition to sustainable energy solutions, INEOS has prioritized innovation in material science, particularly in developing advanced materials that meet the evolving needs of industries such as automotive, construction, and consumer goods. Ratcliffe's emphasis on R&D has driven the creation of high-performance polymers and composites that enhance product performance while reducing weight and environmental impact. For instance, INEOS has developed lightweight materials that improve fuel efficiency in vehicles, thereby contributing to the automotive industry's efforts to reduce emissions.

The commitment to innovation is further exemplified by the establishment of INEOS's Innovation Centre in London. This facility serves as a hub for research and development, where scientists and engineers collaborate to create new technologies and products. The center focuses on cross-disciplinary innovation, bringing together expertise from various fields to tackle complex challenges. By fostering a culture of creativity and collaboration, Ratcliffe has positioned INEOS to remain agile and responsive to market demands.

Ratcliffe's forward-thinking approach extends to digital transformation, recognizing the importance of technology in enhancing operational efficiency and competitiveness. INEOS has embraced digitalization initiatives that leverage data analytics, artificial intelligence, and automation to optimize manufacturing processes and supply chain management. By harnessing these technologies, INEOS can streamline operations, reduce costs, and improve product quality. This commitment to digital innovation is essential in a rapidly evolving industry where efficiency and adaptability are paramount.

Moreover, INEOS has actively engaged in partnerships with technology firms and research institutions to drive innovation further. By collaborating with external experts, INEOS gains access to cutting-edge technologies and ideas that can accelerate its innovation efforts. These partnerships enable the company to stay ahead of industry trends and develop solutions that meet the needs of a diverse customer base. Ratcliffe's openness to collaboration underscores his belief that innovation thrives in environments where knowledge and expertise are shared.

The ongoing push for innovation at INEOS is not limited to energy and materials; it also extends to enhancing overall operational excellence. Ratcliffe has instilled a

Jim Ratcliffe

culture of continuous improvement within the organization, encouraging employees to seek innovative solutions to enhance productivity and efficiency. This culture empowers teams to challenge conventional practices, explore new methodologies, and implement best practices across the organization.

In conclusion, Jim Ratcliffe's leadership at INEOS has positioned the company as a leader in innovation, particularly in the energy sector and beyond. Through a steadfast commitment to sustainability, investments in advanced technologies, and a focus on collaborative partnerships, INEOS is addressing the pressing challenges of today's world while driving growth and competitiveness. Ratcliffe's forward-looking approach to innovation not only enhances INEOS's market position but also contributes to a more sustainable and responsible chemical industry. As the company continues to innovate, it remains poised to meet the demands of a dynamic and evolving global landscape.

Jim Ratcliffe's leadership at INEOS is a testament to his commitment to innovation across the energy sector and

Jim Ratcliffe

beyond, emphasizing the need to address the evolving challenges of sustainability, efficiency, and technological advancement. This multifaceted approach to innovation has propelled INEOS to the forefront of the chemical industry, allowing it to respond effectively to market demands while contributing to global sustainability efforts.

Sustainability Initiatives in Energy

Recognizing the urgent need for cleaner energy solutions, Ratcliffe has prioritized sustainability in INEOS's operations and investments. The company has set ambitious targets to reduce its carbon footprint and transition towards more sustainable energy sources. A key aspect of this strategy is INEOS's investment in hydrogen production. Hydrogen is increasingly being recognized as a vital player in the shift towards decarbonization, and Ratcliffe sees it as an essential element in the future energy landscape.

Jim Ratcliffe

INEOS has embarked on several hydrogen projects, including the development of hydrogen production facilities that utilize innovative technologies to generate low-carbon hydrogen. By focusing on green hydrogen, which is produced through the electrolysis of water using renewable energy, INEOS aims to create a sustainable energy source that can be used across various sectors, including transportation, heating, and industrial processes. These initiatives are designed not only to meet INEOS's internal energy needs but also to provide hydrogen as a service to customers in other industries, thus diversifying its revenue streams.

Additionally, INEOS has explored the potential of blue hydrogen, which is produced from natural gas with carbon capture and storage (CCS) technologies to mitigate emissions. This dual approach allows INEOS to capitalize on existing resources while transitioning towards greener solutions. By investing in hydrogen technology, Ratcliffe has positioned INEOS as a leader in the energy transition, catering to the increasing demand for clean energy solutions.

Jim Ratcliffe

Investments in Bio-Based Feedstocks

As part of its commitment to sustainability, INEOS is also exploring bio-based feedstocks as alternatives to traditional petrochemicals. The company has invested in research and development aimed at creating biofuels and bio-based chemicals that align with the growing consumer demand for sustainable products. This shift not only addresses environmental concerns but also allows INEOS to diversify its product portfolio and reduce its reliance on fossil fuels.

By collaborating with biotech companies and research institutions, INEOS is developing innovative processes for converting biomass into valuable chemicals and fuels. These efforts align with global initiatives to reduce greenhouse gas emissions and promote the use of renewable resources. Ratcliffe's foresight in embracing bio-based solutions positions INEOS to meet the evolving expectations of consumers and regulators alike.

Jim Ratcliffe

Advancements in Material Science

In addition to energy innovations, INEOS has placed a strong emphasis on advancing material science to develop high-performance products that meet the needs of diverse industries. Ratcliffe's vision includes the creation of lightweight materials and specialty chemicals that enhance performance while minimizing environmental impact. For instance, INEOS has focused on developing advanced polymers that reduce weight in automotive applications, thereby improving fuel efficiency and reducing emissions.

This commitment to innovation in materials has led to the creation of products used in various sectors, including automotive, construction, and consumer goods. By investing in R&D for advanced materials, INEOS aims to stay ahead of market trends and respond to the growing demand for sustainable solutions that perform effectively in challenging environments.

Jim Ratcliffe

INEOS's Innovation Centre in London serves as a focal point for these advancements, where multidisciplinary teams work collaboratively to develop new technologies and materials. This facility not only fosters creativity but also serves as a catalyst for cross-industry partnerships, allowing INEOS to leverage external expertise in material science and engineering.

Digital Transformation and Operational Excellence

Jim Ratcliffe has recognized that digital transformation is crucial for enhancing operational efficiency and competitiveness in the chemical industry. INEOS has embraced digital technologies, including data analytics, artificial intelligence, and automation, to optimize manufacturing processes and improve supply chain management. By implementing digital tools, INEOS can monitor production in real-time, identify inefficiencies, and enhance decision-making capabilities.

For example, the integration of predictive maintenance technologies enables INEOS to anticipate equipment failures before they occur, reducing downtime and maintenance costs. This proactive approach not only enhances operational efficiency but also contributes to a safer working environment by minimizing unexpected incidents.

Ratcliffe's commitment to fostering a culture of continuous improvement has empowered employees at all levels to contribute to innovation. By encouraging teams to explore new methodologies and challenge existing practices, INEOS creates an environment conducive to operational excellence. This culture of innovation ensures that INEOS remains adaptable and responsive to the dynamic challenges of the chemical industry.

Collaborative Partnerships and External Engagement

Recognizing that innovation thrives in collaborative environments, Ratcliffe has prioritized partnerships with technology firms, research institutions, and industry stakeholders. By engaging in collaborative projects, INEOS gains access to cutting-edge technologies and insights that accelerate its innovation efforts. These partnerships enable INEOS to stay ahead of industry trends and develop solutions tailored to customer needs.

For instance, INEOS has collaborated with universities on research initiatives focused on sustainable materials and energy technologies. These academic partnerships provide valuable insights into emerging trends and breakthroughs that can enhance INEOS's R&D efforts. Moreover, collaborations with startups and technology firms allow INEOS to tap into innovative ideas and solutions that may not have been possible through internal efforts alone.

Additionally, Ratcliffe has emphasized the importance of engaging with industry associations and initiatives aimed at advancing sustainability in the chemical sector. By participating in collaborative initiatives, INEOS can influence industry standards, share best practices, and contribute to broader sustainability goals. This

Jim Ratcliffe

engagement reflects Ratcliffe's belief in the power of collaboration to drive systemic change within the industry.

Future Outlook and Challenges

As Jim Ratcliffe continues to steer INEOS toward a future defined by innovation, the company faces several challenges inherent in the energy transition and evolving market dynamics. The need to balance profitability with sustainability goals presents a complex challenge, requiring careful navigation

Leadership Philosophy and Management Style

Jim Ratcliffe's leadership philosophy and management style have been pivotal in shaping INEOS into one of the world's leading chemical companies. His approach combines a clear vision, a commitment to innovation, and a focus on operational excellence, all of which have contributed to INEOS's remarkable growth and resilience in a competitive industry. Ratcliffe's leadership is characterized by several core principles that reflect his unique perspective on management and organizational culture.

Visionary Leadership

At the heart of Ratcliffe's leadership philosophy is a visionary mindset that prioritizes long-term goals and strategic thinking. He believes in setting ambitious targets that challenge the status quo, driving the organization towards innovation and growth. Ratcliffe's vision for INEOS is not just about expanding market share; it is about redefining the company's role within the global chemical industry while addressing broader societal challenges, such as sustainability and environmental responsibility. This long-term perspective encourages teams to think beyond immediate gains and consider the lasting impact of their decisions.

Jim Ratcliffe

Decentralized Management Approach

Ratcliffe employs a decentralized management structure that empowers individual business units to operate with a high degree of autonomy. This approach fosters a sense of ownership among managers and employees, encouraging them to take initiative and make decisions that align with the company's overall strategy. By decentralizing decision-making, Ratcliffe enables teams to respond swiftly to market changes and customer needs, creating a more agile organization. This management style not only boosts morale but also enhances operational efficiency, as teams are better equipped to adapt to local conditions and challenges.

Focus on Operational Excellence

A cornerstone of Ratcliffe's management style is his relentless focus on operational excellence. He emphasizes the importance of efficiency, cost-effectiveness, and continuous improvement across

Jim Ratcliffe

all aspects of INEOS's operations. Ratcliffe believes that achieving operational excellence is essential for maintaining a competitive edge in the chemical industry. He encourages a culture of accountability, where employees are expected to identify inefficiencies and propose solutions. This emphasis on operational performance drives teams to optimize processes, reduce waste, and enhance productivity, contributing to INEOS's overall success.

Innovation as a Core Value

Innovation is integral to Ratcliffe's leadership philosophy. He fosters an environment where creativity and experimentation are encouraged, viewing innovation as a vital component of the company's growth strategy. Ratcliffe believes that staying ahead of industry trends and technological advancements is essential for INEOS to remain competitive. He supports investment in research and development, collaboration with external partners, and the exploration of new technologies and materials. By prioritizing innovation, Ratcliffe positions

Jim Ratcliffe

INEOS as a leader in the chemical sector, capable of addressing the evolving needs of customers and the broader market.

Collaboration and Team Empowerment

Ratcliffe champions collaboration and teamwork, recognizing that collective efforts often yield the best results. He fosters a culture where open communication and cross-functional collaboration are valued. Ratcliffe encourages teams to share knowledge and expertise, believing that diverse perspectives contribute to better decision-making and problem-solving. By promoting collaboration, he helps to break down silos within the organization, enabling teams to work together towards common goals.

In addition, Ratcliffe empowers his management team to take ownership of their respective areas, encouraging them to make decisions and drive initiatives. He trusts his leaders to execute their strategies while providing them with the necessary resources and support. This empowerment fosters a sense of responsibility and accountability, motivating employees to perform at their best.

Adaptability and Resilience

In an industry characterized by rapid change and uncertainty, Ratcliffe's leadership style emphasizes adaptability and resilience. He encourages teams to embrace change and view challenges as opportunities for growth. Ratcliffe believes that organizations must be willing to pivot in response to shifting market dynamics and emerging trends. This adaptability is reinforced by a culture of learning, where employees are encouraged to acquire new skills and knowledge to stay relevant in a constantly evolving landscape.

Ratcliffe's resilience is also reflected in his approach to setbacks. He views failures as valuable learning experiences, promoting a mindset where mistakes are acknowledged and analyzed to prevent future occurrences. This attitude fosters an environment of continuous improvement, where employees feel empowered to take risks and innovate without fear of retribution.

Integrity and Ethical Leadership

Integrity is a fundamental aspect of Ratcliffe's leadership philosophy. He believes that ethical behavior and transparency are essential for building trust within the organization and with external stakeholders. Ratcliffe emphasizes the importance of maintaining high ethical standards in all business dealings, promoting a culture of honesty and accountability. He encourages open dialogue about ethical considerations and decision-making processes, ensuring that employees understand the values that underpin INEOS's operations.

Commitment to Sustainability

Ratcliffe's leadership philosophy is closely aligned with a commitment to sustainability and environmental responsibility. He recognizes that the chemical industry

Jim Ratcliffe

faces increasing scrutiny regarding its environmental impact, and he is determined to position INEOS as a responsible corporate citizen. Under his leadership, INEOS has embraced sustainability as a core value, investing in initiatives aimed at reducing carbon emissions, advancing recycling technologies, and developing bio-based products.

This commitment to sustainability not only reflects Ratcliffe's personal values but also resonates with customers and investors who prioritize responsible business practices. By integrating sustainability into the company's strategy, Ratcliffe enhances INEOS's reputation and long-term viability in a changing market landscape.

Jim Ratcliffe's leadership philosophy and management style have been instrumental in shaping INEOS into a leading global chemical company. His visionary approach, focus on operational excellence, commitment to innovation, and emphasis on collaboration and integrity create a dynamic organizational culture that drives growth and adaptability. By fostering an

Jim Ratcliffe

environment that empowers employees, encourages creativity, and prioritizes sustainability, Ratcliffe has positioned INEOS for continued success in a competitive industry. As the company navigates the challenges of the future, Ratcliffe's leadership principles will undoubtedly guide INEOS toward new opportunities and milestones.

Jim Ratcliffe

CONCLUSION

In conclusion, *Jim Ratcliffe: The Industrialist Behind INEOS* captures the remarkable story of a man who defied conventional business wisdom to create one of the largest privately-owned companies in the world. From his early days in Failsworth, through his time in chemical engineering and finance, to his bold ventures with INEOS, Ratcliffe's career has been defined by audacity, innovation, and an unrelenting drive for success.

Ratcliffe's journey illustrates the power of resilience, adaptability, and strategic thinking in building a global empire. His ability to turn underperforming industries into profitable enterprises and navigate economic shifts while maintaining a vision for long-term growth sets him apart as a transformative figure in business. Beyond chemicals, his ventures into sports, adventure, and philanthropy highlight his diverse interests and willingness to embrace new challenges.

Jim Ratcliffe

Ultimately, Ratcliffe's legacy is not just about the wealth and power he has accumulated but about how he has redefined modern industrialism through a fearless approach to business. His story is a testament to the rewards of calculated risk, visionary leadership, and an unwavering commitment to success, leaving an enduring mark on industries worldwide. As the world continues to evolve, Jim Ratcliffe remains a pivotal figure, shaping the future of global enterprise with the same ingenuity and determination that have driven his extraordinary life.

www.ingramcontent.com/pod-product-compliance
Lightning Source LLC
Chambersburg PA
CBHW071102240526
45471CB00016B/2406